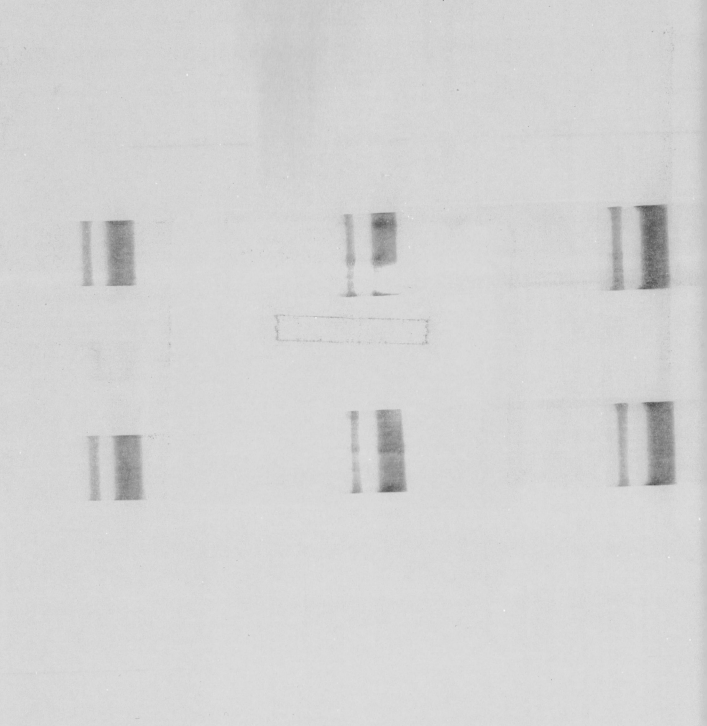

MARVELS and MYSTERIES

UFOS and CROP CIRCLES

Paul Mason

Smart Apple Media

This edition first published in 2005 in the United States of America by Smart Apple Media.

Smart Apple Media
1980 Lookout Drive
North Mankato
Minnesota 56003

First published in 2005 by
MACMILLAN EDUCATION AUSTRALIA PTY LTY
627 Chapel Street, South Yarra, Australia 3141

Visit our website at www.macmillan.com.au

Associated companies and representatives throughout the world.

Library of Congress Cataloging-in-Publication Data

Mason, Paul, 1967-
    UFO's and crop circles / by Paul Mason.
    p. cm. – (Marvels and mysteries)
    Includes index.

    ISBN 1-58340-787-1

    1. Unidentified flying objects—Sightings and encounters—Juvenile literature. 2. Crop circles—Juvenile literature. I. Title.
    CL789.2.M3685 2005
    001.942—dc22

                                                        2005042865

Edited by Vanessa Lanaway
Text and cover design by Karen Young
Page layout by Karen Young
Illustrations by Jacqui Grantford
Maps and diagram on p.11 by Karen Young
Photo research by Jes Senbergs

Printed in China

Acknowledgments

The author and the publisher are grateful to the following for permission to reproduce copyright material:

Front cover photograph: Artist's impression of UFO over Rendlesham Forest, courtesy of Fortean Picture Library/Philippa Foster.

Texture used in cover and pages, courtesy of Photodisc.

Corbis, pp. 9, 13, 15, 18, 20, 23; Fortean Picture Library, pp. 8, 12, 17, 19, 22, 24, 26, 27, 28; Fortean Picture Library/Bob Skinner, p. 21; Fortean Picture Library/Dennis Stacy, p. 14; Chris Ware/Getty Images, p. 7; Mary Evans Picture Library, pp. 4, 6, 10; Photolibrary.com, pp. 5, 25; Stockbyte, p. 29; Pearlie Tan, p. 16.

While every care has been taken to trace and acknowledge copyright, the publisher tenders their apologies for any accidental infringement where copyright has proved untraceable. Where the attempt has been unsuccessful, the publisher welcomes information that would redress the situation.

CONTENTS

GLOSSARY WORDS

When a word is printed in **bold**, you can look up its meaning in the glossary words box, and on page 31.

TIME

Some of the stories in this book talk about things that happened a long time ago, even more than 2,000 years ago. To understand this, people measure time in years Before the Common Era (BCE) and during the Common Era (CE). It looks like this on a timeline:

2000 1500 1000 500   0   500 1000 1500 2000 2500

Years BCE   **Years CE**

What is a UFO?

The letters **UFO** stand for **U**nidentified **F**lying **O**bject. In theory, anything that flies can be called a UFO, if the person looking at it does not know what it is. In reality, when people talk about UFOs they usually mean craft that are carrying "visitors" from outer space.

When were the first UFOs sighted?

Some writers suggest that UFOs have been visiting Earth for thousands of years. People claimed to have seen a giant shield in the skies of Ancient Rome in 216 BCE. However, UFOs did not become really common until soon after World War II, in 1947.

The world's first UFO "craze" began in 1947. Within days of the first sighting, newspapers and magazines began to publish UFO articles. Soon, specialist magazines and books began to appear.

FACT FILE

Close encounters

Investigators put encounters between humans and UFOs into five different categories, called close encounters.

Close encounter 1: A simple sighting.

Close encounter 2: The UFO has an effect, such as causing lights to go out.

Close encounter 3: The aliens inside the UFO are seen.

Close encounter 4: The aliens **abduct** the person who has seen their craft.

Close encounter 5: Humans deliberately communicate with the aliens.

What do UFOs look like?

Various kinds of UFOs have been reported. One of the most common is the "flying saucer," a disc-shaped craft. People have also claimed to see UFOs shaped like giant cigars, huge flying wedges, massive lanterns, and simply mysterious lights in the sky.

UFO sightings continue to be common today. Some areas seem especially likely to be visited by UFOs. This photo was taken in Gulf Breeze, Florida. Hundreds of UFO encounters were reported there after a sighting in 1987.

FACT FILE

Alien types

Humanoid: Humanoid aliens are said to look like people. The most commonly reported humanoids today are "grays" — small, gray-skinned aliens with bald heads, and almond-shaped eyes.

Animal: These aliens look more like animals, often reptiles.

Robot: Robot aliens seem to be machines.

Exotic: Exotic aliens seem to be fantasy creatures, not recognized as anything familiar.

LOCATION FILE

Date: September 3, 1965

Location: near town of Exeter, New Hampshire.

Details: Multiple witnesses, including a police officer, see a UFO in the skies near Exeter. The UFO chases cars and examines houses before disappearing.

Explanation: not known.

GLOSSARY WORDS

abduct   take someone away against their will

The FOO FIGHTERS

Location: Germany and the Truk Lagoon, Pacific Ocean
Date: 1944

The foo fighters were the first modern UFOs. They were spotted in 1944, during World War II. The foo fighters began to appear near **Allied** bomber and fighter planes. No one could explain what they were.

What did the foo fighters look like?

The foo fighters were small, flying balls of light. The lights were red, gold, or white. Sometimes they would blink on and off. The foo fighters appeared alone, in pairs, or in groups. They could fly at very high speed. Strangest of all, they did not appear on **radar** screens.

Because no foo fighter was ever tracked by radar, it was impossible to know their exact speed. They were clearly very fast, though. Reports claimed that the foo fighters were able to fly between 200 and 500 miles (320 and 800 km) per hour.

 Foo fighters may have been created in German experimental research laboratories.

What were the foo fighters?

Two facts helped experts to guess the likely identity of the foo fighters. Firstly, they usually appeared near Allied bombing routes. They also disappeared when the Allies captured German experimental research laboratories. These facts suggest that the foo fighters were probably devices aimed at confusing Allied radar, rather than visitors from outer space.

GLOSSARY WORDS

Allied   the group of countries that won World War II, including the U.S., UK, Australia, and New Zealand

radar   a device for seeing aircraft from a long way away

The first FLYING SAUCERS

Location: Cascade Mountains, U.S.
Date: June 24, 1947

The first ever UFO craze began in 1947. American pilot Kenneth Arnold spotted a group of objects traveling at an incredible speed. They moved faster than any aircraft known at the time. No one could explain what the objects were.

Arnold had been flying alone over the Cascade Mountains in the U.S. He spotted a group of nine UFOs flying between two mountain peaks. Arnold made a rough calculation of their speed. They seemed to be moving about 1,200 miles (1,900 km) per hour!

Arnold with a painting of one of the saucers, painted long after he first spotted them. By this time, his descriptions of the saucers had changed a little, giving them a more "plane-like" shape.

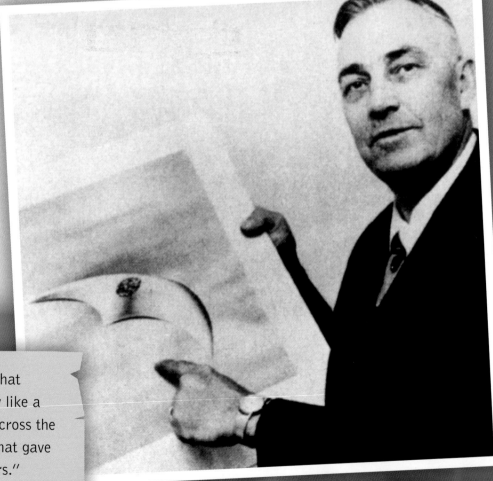

8

 A Northrop XB-35

 A Northrop XB-35

Was it a plane?

Two experimental planes have been put forward as possible explanations for the Arnold UFOs. Remember that Arnold said he had seen nine UFOs.

- The Northrop XB-35: only two existed, and neither was flying on June 24, 1947.

- The Ho IX: this was a single plane brought back from Germany at the end of World War II. However, the Ho IX almost certainly never flew.

What did the UFOs look like?

Arnold gave a clear description of the UFOs. He said they looked like "a pie plate that was cut in half." They also had some sort of triangle at the back. Arnold said he had only been able to see the UFOs clearly when they dipped their wings and shone in the sunlight.

Invaders from the air?

Kenneth Arnold's UFO encounter in 1947 caused a panic in the U.S. Within days, UFO sightings had been reported in 39 different states. People were worried that America was threatened by its enemy, the **USSR**. They feared that America could soon be under attack.

People were scared by the idea of the USSR having aircraft that could fly quicker than any American jet. In a way, it was probably less frightening for them to think that such craft were from outer space.

In the 1990s, it began to seem that Kenneth Arnold had not seen UFOs in 1947. By that time, though, there had been thousands of other UFO sightings. There were movies, magazines, websites—a whole UFO industry had appeared.

65661

UFO REVIEW

No. 7
$1.00

SPECIAL "WOULD YOU BELIEVE?" SUPPLEMENT

The World's Only Flying Saucer Newspaper

MASSIVE UFO LANDINGS TO TAKE PLACE
WILL YOU BE TAKEN ONBOARD BY THE ALIENS?

LANDGRAF

07

74470 65661

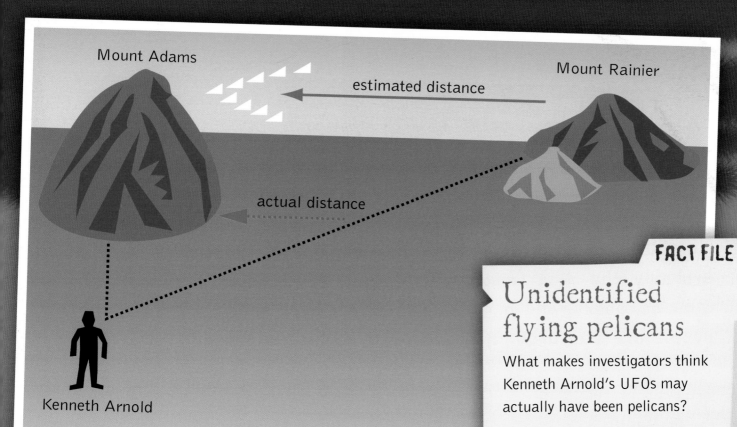

Mount Adams

Mount Rainier

estimated distance

actual distance

Kenneth Arnold

Arnold thought the objects flew from Mount Rainier to Mount Adams in less than two minutes. He thought they must be UFOs to cover that distance so quickly. However, they were actually closer to Arnold than he thought, so they didn't fly as far, or as fast.

Unidentified flying pelicans

What makes investigators think Kenneth Arnold's UFOs may actually have been pelicans?

- The birds have a **wingspan** of up to 10 feet (3 m) and fly at high **altitudes**.

- They travel in the "skipping" motion Arnold described.

- Their wings are dazzlingly white when caught in the light.

- When gliding, pelicans are a similar shape to the UFOs Arnold described.

What were the UFOs?

It is unlikely that the UFOs Kenneth Arnold saw were alien visitors. They were not from the USSR, either. In fact, they were almost certainly a group of American White Pelicans! New investigations make it seem likely that the "UFOs" were actually closer to Arnold than he guessed. This led him to be wrong about their speed— and it was their speed that first made people think the craft might be UFOs.

GLOSSARY WORDS

USSR — the Union of Soviet Socialist Republics, a country led by what is now Russia. The USSR was a "superpower" rival to the U.S. from about 1947 to 1990.

wingspan — the distance from wingtip to wingtip

altitudes — heights above sea level

The ROSWELL incident

Location: Roswell, New Mexico, U.S.
Date: June 1947

The "UFO landing" at Roswell, New Mexico in 1947 is probably the most famous ever. It has led to magazine articles, books, and a whole TV series. Even today, people are still arguing about what really happened.

Crash in a field

On June 14, 1947, a rancher discovered strange **wreckage** in one of his fields. Soon after, the rancher went into town and heard about the Arnold UFO sighting. He began to wonder if the wreckage in his field might be a crashed UFO.

A newspaper article reporting the discovery of the Roswell wreckage, by a rancher named Jesse Brazel. At first he thought it was a weather balloon. Two of these had crashed nearby before. Then Brazel began to reconsider—perhaps there was more wreckage than from other crashed balloons? He started to wonder if he had found a crashed UFO.

Roswell Daily Record

RAAF Captures Flying Saucer On Ranch in Roswell Region

FACT FILE

Roswell High

The Roswell incident was the inspiration behind a cult TV show in the 1990s.

- The show was called "Roswell" after the school its characters went to.

- In it, the teenage descendants of aliens live among the humans of Roswell.

The town of Roswell is famous for the wreckage that was discovered there. People take tours to visit the crash site.

What was the wreckage like?

The army sent two officers to investigate the Roswell wreckage. They collected pieces and took them back to the local air base. Then, on July 8, the local newspaper carried an amazing story. "The intelligence office... at Roswell Army Air Force Base announced at noon today that the field has come into possession of a flying saucer."

GLOSSARY WORDS

wreckage   the broken-up parts of something that has crashed

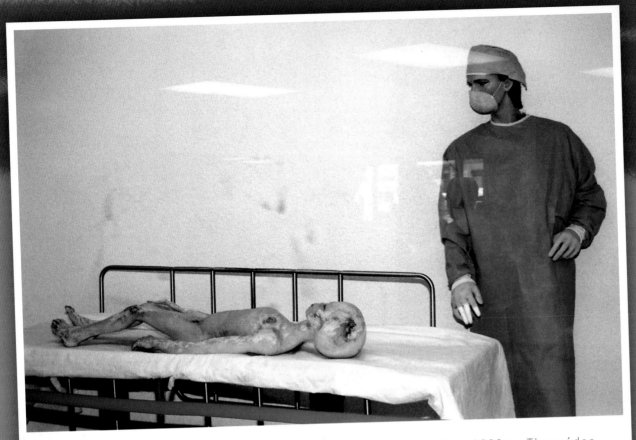

This display recreates a video that appeared in the 1990s. The video claimed to show the bodies of Roswell "aliens" being examined in secret. It was quickly discovered to be a **hoax**.

What crashed at Roswell?

Investigators tried for years to discover exactly what it was that crashed near Roswell in 1947. One difficulty was that the U.S. government refused to release any information. This allowed all sorts of wild rumors to begin.

Some people even suggested that the bodies of small aliens had been found in the wreckage. These were **allegedly** taken to the air base, then smuggled away in children's coffins. In fact, the coffins people saw were probably being used to smuggle alcohol in and out, not alien bodies.

The mystery unravels

The U.S. government's secret listening device, Project Mogul, could be the mystery craft that crashed at Roswell.

- Mogul Flight 4 left Alamagordo air base, not far from Roswell, on June 4.

- Mogul used advanced equipment that would have looked unfamiliar to the people who saw it.

- Because Mogul was top secret, the government refused to release any information about it. This allowed rumors of a UFO crash to spread.

What was Project Mogul?

Project Mogul was a top-secret device belonging to the U.S. government. It was designed to listen for nuclear explosions in the USSR. It floated high in the atmosphere using a string of 23 weather balloons. It now seems likely that Mogul Flight 4 crashed near Roswell. Its unusual equipment confused people into thinking it came from outer space.

Parts of the Roswell wreckage are said to have been covered in alien writing. In fact, this was probably tape covered in a flower-like pattern. It had been used by a New York toy company that made radar reflectors for Project Mogul.

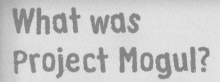

GLOSSARY WORDS

hoax — an imitation of something, designed to fool people into thinking it is real

allegedly — claimed to be true by some people, but not proven

The Valentich DISAPPEARANCE

Location: Bass Strait, Australia
Date: October 21, 1978

The mysterious case of Fred Valentich continues to puzzle investigators today. He disappeared while flying over Bass Strait in Australia. Valentich's last message seemed to show that he had been **"buzzed"** – and perhaps destroyed–by a UFO.

Valentich set off from Melbourne, Australia, on October 21, 1978, heading for King Island. At 7.06 P.M., he contacted Melbourne airfield, saying that a large aircraft had passed very close to his plane. Then the aircraft started to hover over him. Valentich began to experience engine trouble.

Valentich in trouble

Valentich described the thing that was following him as having "a long shape" and then decided, "it's not an aircraft." The people at Melbourne airfield could not identify it, and it did not appear on their radar screen. Valentich's last message was his **call-sign**, followed by 17 seconds of loud metallic screeching. He was never heard from or seen again.

Fred Valentich was 20 years old and a qualified pilot when he set out alone to fly across Bass Strait. He reported being followed by a UFO of some sort, with "a green light and a sort of metallic light outside." Then his plane disappeared forever. A memorial plaque has been placed at Cape Otway lighthouse, which looks out over Bass Strait.

MELBOURNE EPISODE

CASE STUDY OF A MISSING PILOT

Richard F. Haines

Bass Strait mysteries

The Valentich disappearance is not the only Bass Strait mystery.

- In July 1977, the Cape Otway lighthouse-keeper and others saw a brilliant white light hovering over the sea.

- In February 1944, a bomber was trailed by a UFO, which eventually raced away at about 700 miles (1,100 km) per hour.

- In October 1935, a mail plane carrying 12 passengers disappeared without a trace.

- In July 1920, a schooner disappeared. When a search plane was sent to investigate, it also disappeared.

◄···· This story of Fred Valentich's disappearance was published in 1987.

MINI FACT

The same day as Fred Valentich disappeared, there were many reports of UFOs being seen. Between midday and 9 P.M., there were six sightings in Victoria, and one on King Island. A further eight sightings were reported elsewhere in southeast Australia.

GLOSSARY WORDS

buzzed   overtaken quickly, especially in the air

call-sign   the group of letters that pilots use to identify themselves and their plane on the radio

The Sorrell Lake SAUCERS

Location: Sorrell Lake, Tasmania, Australia
Date: February 26, 1975

In 1975, two men camping in a remote area of Tasmania were amazed to be disturbed by flying saucers. Other witnesses also saw the saucers, but no one was able to explain what they were.

The saucers first appeared at about 8.45 P.M. Each had a red, **pulsing** light in the center and other lights around the edge. One of the saucers approached, and the men saw that it was about 200 feet (60 m) wide. A brilliant beam of light came from the saucer. It appeared to search an area called Robinson's Swamp before whizzing away at high speed.

MINI FACT

The witnesses to the Sorrell Lake saucers did not want to be named. Often UFO spotters have been accused of making up stories to get **publicity** or attention. This was not so in the case of the Sorrell Lake saucers.

LOCATION FILE

Location: Tasmania, Australia

Name: Sorrell Lake

Another UFO was spotted at Sorrell Lake within a few weeks of the first. On March 14, 1975, a group of five campers saw a football-shaped UFO rise up out of the trees and disappear.

Other witnesses

The next day, other witnesses came forward. A group of fishermen had been camping about a mile away. They were inside their tent when suddenly the saucer's beam had lit it up "like daylight." They too were unable to explain what they had seen. To this day, it remains a mystery.

The Balwyn photo

A Melbourne businessman apparently took this famous photo on April 2, 1966. The man claimed it showed a UFO. But is it real?

• The chimney in the bottom-left is more faded than the UFO.

• The photo shows a jagged line along the middle.

The photo is almost certainly a fake. Two photos have been stuck together, then re-photographed to make one.

GLOSSARY WORDS

pulsing — growing stronger then weaker over and over again

publicity — attention in the newspapers or on television

CROP CIRCLES

Location: South-west England
Date: from 1980 onward

Crop circles are mysterious patterns that appear in the middle of fields of wheat. The wheat is squashed down flat over a large area, with no trace of how it happened. Many people have suggested that crop circles show where UFOs have landed.

The first crop circles appeared in 1980 in Wiltshire, England. They were plain oval shapes. In 1983 the circles began to look more complicated. The newspapers took notice, and interest in crop circles grew.

 The stone circle at Avebury, Wiltshire has always been the site of strange legends. One story says that if you run around a stone named the Devil's Chair a hundred times **"widdershins,"** Satan himself will appear.

LOCATION FILE

Location: Wiltshire, England

Name: Weird Wiltshire

Wiltshire must be one of the spookiest areas in England. Ghosts, crop circles, mysterious creatures, UFOs—Wiltshire has them all! It is also home to two famous ancient stone circles, Stonehenge and Avebury.

What were the crop circles?

Dr. Terence Meaden thought he could explain the circles. Meaden was a scientist researching tornados and storms. He said the circles were caused by mini **whirlwinds**, which sprang up and flattened the crops.

The wind theory seemed a good one until the circles began to get even more complicated. By 1990, images of animals and whales had begun to appear. These could not have been created by whirlwinds.

Through the 1980s the crop circles of Wiltshire got more and more complicated. Animal designs began to appear. Some people claimed these were warnings that the Earth was being poisoned by pollution.

GLOSSARY WORDS

widdershins   an old word for counterclockwise

whirlwinds   powerful currents of circling air

Explaining the circles

By 1990, the crop circles were attracting crowds of people. Some farmers were even charging people to see "their" crop circles. Arguments continued to rage about what caused the crop circles to appear.

In 1991, two men claimed that they had made the circles. They had seen similar ones in Queensland, Australia in 1966. The men had recreated the circles for fun. When people began to say the circles were made by the wind, the hoaxers made them increasingly complicated. This was to prove the wind was not responsible.

Evidence from Queensland

An investigator went to Queensland to see if she could discover crop circles there. It turned out that many circles had been seen. They appeared among the reeds in the swamps south of Cairns. So the hoaxers' story was probably true. The complicated crop circles in Wiltshire were made by humans, not UFOs. Some simple ones were probably made by the wind, just like those in Queensland.

Even simple circles such as these are too perfect to have been made by the wind. But they were based on wind-created circles seen in Queensland, Australia.

22

Once the crop circles of Wiltshire began to become famous, circles were spotted all around the world. This one is from California, U.S. Crop circles continue to be seen. In 2001, 184 were reported worldwide.

FACT FILE

Historical crop circles

Investigations have uncovered evidence of ancient crop circles:

• In the 1800s people had actually seen the circles appearing.

• Accounts from the 1500s suggested that the circles were the work of the Devil.

The RENDLESHAM landings

Location: Rendlesham Forest, Suffolk, England
Date: December 27–30, 1980

Several mysterious UFO encounters took place in Rendlesham Forest, England. Airmen from nearby U.S. air bases witnessed mysterious craft hovering over the ground and flying in the night sky. Many people saw the UFOs, which also appeared on radar.

On December 27, **sentries** at the Woodbridge air base reported that they had seen odd white lights in the forest. Three men went to investigate. They came back saying that they had seen a UFO, either hovering above the ground or resting on thin legs.

····▷ The Rendlesham UFO seen on December 27 was said to be metallic, and triangular in shape. Witnesses said it was about 10 feet (3 m) across the bottom, and about 7 feet (2 m) high. It gave off a white light that lit the surrounding area clearly.

December 28–29 landings

On December 28–29, more strange lights were seen in the forest. This time they were red, not white. A group was sent to investigate. The object in the trees seemed to break up and disappear. Immediately, three bright lights appeared in the sky. One headed south, beaming down rays of light as it went. No one could explain what had happened.

When the UFO "landing site" was examined, three depressions were found in the ground. Scientists also found traces of radiation on the ground and on the sides of trees facing the clearing.

Possible explanations

Several possible explanations for what was seen in Rendlesham Forest have been put forward:

• Some people say it was the nearby Orford Ness lighthouse, seen through the trees. But this does not explain how the light moved about.

• Others suggest that **depressions** found in the ground were really rabbit burrows, not marks made by a landing UFO. But this does not explain why they were found to be radioactive.

GLOSSARY WORDS

sentries	armed guards watching for enemies or intruders
depressions	dips or shallow holes in the ground

The landings continue

The mysterious events in Rendlesham Forest continued for another night. Something yellow began to approach through the woods. It seemed to be releasing **luminous** pieces. Another UFO was spotted hovering over Woodbridge. The UFO appeared to be beaming down rays of light.

Rendlesham rumors

Although the **military** tried to keep events quiet, word soon got out. Strange rumors began to circulate. Some people claimed that the base commander, General Gordon Williams, had met three aliens. The aliens were said to have appeared from a beam of light, which came from their UFO. No evidence has ever been found to prove that this really happened.

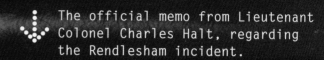

The official memo from Lieutenant Colonel Charles Halt, regarding the Rendlesham incident.

DEPARTMENT OF THE AIR FORCE
HEADQUARTERS 81ST COMBAT SUPPORT GROUP (USAFE)
APO NEW YORK 09755

13 Jan 81

CD

Unexplained Lights

RAF/CC

1. Early in the morning of 27 Dec 80 (approximately 0300L), two USAF security police patrolmen saw unusual lights outside the back gate at RAF Woodbridge. Thinking an aircraft might have crashed or been forced down, they called for permission to go outside the gate to investigate. The on-duty flight chief responded and allowed three patrolmen to proceed on foot. The individuals reported seeing a strange glowing object in the forest. The object was described as being metalic in appearance and triangular in shape, approximately two to three meters across the base and approximately two meters high. It illuminated the entire forest with a white light. The object itself had a pulsing red light on top and a bank(s) of blue lights underneath. The object was hovering or on legs. As the patrolmen approached the object, it maneuvered through the trees and disappeared. At this time the animals on a nearby farm went into a frenzy. The object was briefly sighted approximately an hour later near the back gate.

2. The next day, three depressions 1 1/2" deep and 7" in diameter were found where the object had been sighted on the ground. The following night (29 Dec 80) the area was checked for radiation. Beta/gamma readings of 0.1 milliroentgens were recorded with peak readings in the three depressions and near the center of the triangle formed by the depressions. A nearby tree had moderate (.05-.07) readings on the side of the tree toward the depressions.

3. Later in the night a red sun-like light was seen through the trees. It moved about and pulsed. At one point it appeared to throw off glowing particles and then broke into five separate white objects and then disappeared. Immediately thereafter, three star-like objects were noticed in the sky, two objects to the north and one to the south, all of which were about 10° off the horizon. The objects moved rapidly in sharp angular movements and displayed red, green and blue lights. The objects to the north appeared to be elliptical through an 8-12 power lens. They then turned to full circles. The objects to the north remained in the sky for an hour or more. The object to the south was visible for two or three hours and beamed down a stream of light from time to time. Numerous individuals, including the undersigned, witnessed the activities in paragraphs 2 and 3.

CHARLES I. HALT, Lt Col, USAF
Deputy Base Commander

What landed at Rendlesham?

No one is sure what landed in the forest during December 1980. But many observers agree that something unexplained was going on. As well as the accounts of many witnesses, there is physical evidence. This includes damage to trees, traces of radioactivity, and the fact that at least one UFO appeared on radar.

LOCATION FILE

Date: 1989–90

Location: Belgium

Details: Flying "triangles" are first spotted by two policemen. Hundreds of reports are finally made of similar UFOs in the skies above Belgium. There is no known explanation for these sightings.

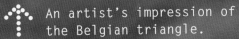

An artist's impression of the Belgian triangle.

GLOSSARY WORDS

luminous	glowing in the dark
military	armed forces, the army, navy, or air force
civilians	people who are not members of the army, navy, or air force

UFOs
over New Zealand

One of the greatest UFO mysteries of all time unfolded in the skies of New Zealand. As well as being visible, the UFOs appeared on radar screens. Something was definitely up there. To this day, though, no one has been able to explain what the UFOs were.

On the night of December 21, 1978 a **cargo plane** reported that a UFO had come towards it at "tremendous speed." The object had traveled 15 miles (24 km) in five seconds, which is a speed of 10,700 miles (17,280 km) per hour. Word of the UFO encounter soon began to spread.

Filming the UFO

On December 31, a film crew joined the same cargo flight. They were planning to make a report about what had happened on December 21. Instead, they were able to film an encounter with several UFOs. Throughout the trip their plane met brightly lit UFOs moving at incredible speeds. Everyone was glad to get safely back to Earth.

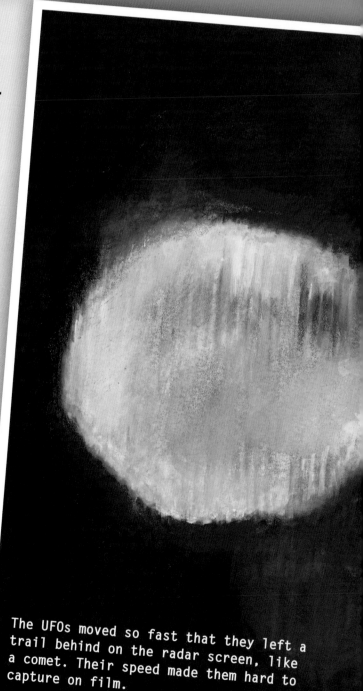

The UFOs moved so fast that they left a trail behind on the radar screen, like a comet. Their speed made them hard to capture on film.

The 1959 UFO

The story of another famous UFO encounter comes from New Zealand:

- On July 13, 1959, at 5.30 A.M., a woman going to milk her cows was scared by two green lights shining through the clouds.

- She ran away, but turned back to see two beings inside a flying saucer that hovered above the ground. The saucer soon rose into the clouds at incredible speed and disappeared.

- There were no other witnesses to these events.

GLOSSARY WORDS

cargo plane   an airplane that carries goods

UFO
timeline

1944–5	Foo fighters spotted in the skies of western Europe and the Pacific Ocean.
1946	Mysterious "ghost rockets" reported in Scandinavia.
1947	June 24: Kenneth Arnold reports flying saucers in Washington State. July 8: The *Roswell Daily Record* reports that the army has recovered flying saucer wreckage from a field near Roswell, New Mexico.
1951	U.S. Air Force begins Project Blue Book, a file on UFO sightings in the U.S. and near U.S. air bases overseas.
1959	A woman in New Zealand sees a UFO when going to milk her cows.
1964	From 1964 onward, the "Warminster Thing" appears near the town of Warminster, England.
1965	UFOs are reported in Exeter, New Hampshire.
1966	The "Balwyn photo" apparently shows a UFO over Melbourne, Australia. It later seems likely to be a fake. Doug Bower and Dave Chorley see crop circles in Queensland, Australia. They later fake similar circles back home in England.
1975	February 26: UFOs reported over Sorrell Lake, Tasmania, Australia.
1978	October 21: Fred Valentich disappears while flying alone across Bass Strait, Australia after reporting contact with a UFO. December 21–31: UFOs are filmed over New Zealand, near the city of Wellington.
1980	December 27–30: reports of UFO activity near U.S. air bases close to Rendlesham Forest, Suffolk, England. Crop circles begin to be noticed in Wiltshire, England.
1983	Crop circles become a worldwide phenomenon.
1989	A wave of UFO sightings begins in Belgium.
1990	Second wave of UFO sightings in Belgium.
1991	Crop circle hoaxers Doug Bower and Dave Chorley come forward and admit that they created many of the crop circles people claimed were UFO landing sites.
1997	There are multiple sightings of UFOs in the skies over Phoenix, Arizona.

GLOSSARY

abduct take someone away against their will

allegedly claimed to be true by some people, but not proven

Allied the group of countries that won World War II, including the U.S., UK, Australia, and New Zealand

altitudes heights above sea level

buzzed overtaken quickly, especially in the air

call-sign the group of letters that pilots use to identify themselves and their plane on the radio

cargo plane an airplane that carries goods

civilians people who are not members of the army, navy, or air force

depressions dips or shallow holes in the ground

hoax an imitation of something, designed to fool people into thinking it is real

luminous glowing in the dark

military armed forces, the army, navy, or air force

publicity attention in the newspapers or on television

pulsing growing stronger then weaker over and over again

radar a device for seeing aircraft from a long way away

sentries armed guards watching for enemies or intruders

USSR the Union of Soviet Socialist Republics, a country led by what is now Russia. The USSR was a "superpower" rival to the U.S. from about 1947 to 1990.

whirlwinds powerful currents of circling air

widdershins an old word for counterclockwise

wingspan the distance from wingtip to wingtip

wreckage the broken-up parts of something that has crashed

INDEX